"If women work together, their field for activity is unlimited."

From Mrs. Driscoll's speech at a dinner on October 3, 1939, prior to Clara Driscoll Day, an honor proclaimed by Governor W. Lee O'Daniel.

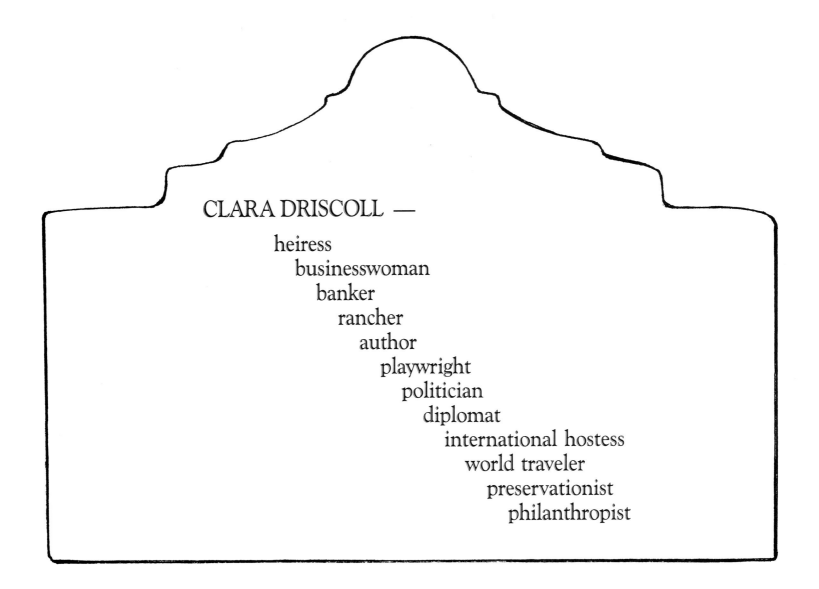

CLARA DRISCOLL —

heiress
businesswoman
banker
rancher
author
playwright
politician
diplomat
international hostess
world traveler
preservationist
philanthropist

Mrs. Driscoll dressed with flair and elegance. The costumes sketched are from photographs which reflect her fashion taste.

The cover design is adapted from the rose window, Mission San Jose, San Antonio. This motif was featured in Laguna Gloria, her Austin home.

The narrative and the pictorial history are composed as a scrapbook, reminiscent of her way of recording interests, travels, and organizational activities.

"Search the histories of the world and you will not find a deed to equal that of the men who died within the Alamo that Texas might be free . . ."

From Clara Driscoll's book, *In the Shadow of the Alamo*, published in 1906.

Clara Driscoll's Story

I was born April 2, 1881, in St. Mary's, a small town on the South Texas coast. My father, Robert Driscoll, Sr., owned and operated a large ranch which he called Palo Alto. Here I learned to speak Spanish, to ride horses, and to rope cattle.

My parents sent me to private schools in San Antonio, New York, and Paris. I studied French, German, literature, and the arts. In 1898 I was vacationing in Spain when the Spanish-American War broke out. I was seventeen, and this was too interesting an opportunity for me to resist. I assumed a Spanish name, pretended to be a native, and remained for six months to observe developments. I then returned to the Chateau Dieudonne to finish my formal education in May of 1899 when I was eighteen.

After graduation, my mother, who had traveled with me in many countries, was to accompany me home. On our stopover in London, however, Mother suddenly became ill and died. Shocked and bereft, I returned home to my father and my brother Robert, ten years my senior.

continued on Plate 1

Plate 1

From my Irish father I inherited a firm chin. People said that my auburn hair and reddish brown eyes matched my fiery temperament. This was aroused at the sight of the crumbling Missions in San Antonio, a city I visited frequently. Becoming even more upset over plans to build a hotel next to the Alamo Chapel, that shrine of heroes, I joined the Daughters of the Republic of Texas in an attempt to save the ground where Travis and his brave men had died. We received some contributions, including the pennies of school children. Unfortunately, we fell far short of the $75,000 needed to purchase the site adjoining the Chapel.

After graduation, girls in the 1890's wore their hair done up instead of long. A tight, strapless corset gave my figure an hour-glass shape. My petticoats were stiffly starched.

Corset cover and petticoat   Combination and corset   School days robe and gown

Plate 2

(Courtesy, Gonzales County Archives)

The Alamo in 1903

In 1903 I appeared before the Texas Legislature to ask the State to buy the historic ground, but time had run out. Before the House and Senate could meet in 1905, the full purchase price had to be paid. There was no one to put up the payment except me.

After years of struggle, we women were overjoyed when both Houses in the State Capitol voted to purchase the property from me and to make the Daughters of the Republic of Texas custodians of it. The State repaid me. I continued to provide support so that visitors might enjoy the Alamo and the grounds free of charge.

School days travel suit

With the Texas Press at the Alamo, 1904.

Plate 3

I was honored to be queen of the San Antonio Fiesta three times: in 1904, 1905, and 1906.

This celebration paid tribute to the heroes of the Alamo and the Battle of San Jacinto at which General Sam Houston and the Texian rebels defeated General Santa Anna and the Mexican troops in 1836. My own grandfathers fought with Houston.

In the Fiesta parade my carriage was decorated with roses. Flowers were tossed in a mock battle which gave the event its name, "Battle of Flowers."

Ball gown and cape

Plate 4

In each parade I carried a parasol which matched my gown. A fan was part of my evening wear when I attended the Fiesta balls.

Plate 5

When I pleaded with the Texas Legislature to support the Alamo cause, I met Henry Hulme Sevier, State Representative from Uvalde. Hal was a young, handsome, charming Southern gentleman. Our friendship developed over a period of three years.

During this time, in my early twenties, I wrote books and plays. I especially enjoyed writing the story and lyrics for a muscial I called *Mexicana*. This comic opera opened on Broadway in 1906 as a production of the Schubert Brothers. The cast, scenery, and costumes were the best that could be obtained in New York and Europe.

Costumes worn by *Mexicana* dancers

Caro Roma, star of the show.

Plate 6

In July of 1906, Hal and I were married in St. Patrick's Cathedral in New York City. We sailed to Europe for a three-months' wedding trip which included sight-seeing in Italy and Paris, and theater evenings in London.

It was fashionable for women attending the theater to wear elaborate hats. These had to be pinned to the seat backs; otherwise, people sitting behind could not see the performance!

Travel suit, 1906

Plate 7

When Hal and I returned from Europe we lived in New York. We built a home in the Oyster Bay area of Long Island. Our neighbors were our longtime friends, the Theodore Roosevelt family. While Hal worked as financial editor of the New York *Sun*, I helped to organize the Texas Club. It was the first state club in the city to include women as active members and office holders. We planned delightful dinner parties and dances based on Lone Star themes.

Harem costume for a party

Texas Club Military Dinner and
Favor Dance at the Plaza, 1912

Plate 8

Hal and I moved back to Texas when my dear father died in 1914. Hal founded his own newspaper, the Austin *American.*

Our second dream home was built in Austin near a lagoon. We called this house Laguna Gloria. Here we entertained guests from everywhere.

Many Texas clubwomen were my friends, and most called me "Miss Clara." Once a group of them met at our home, and I took them on a tour of the Rio Grande Valley and Palo Alto.

Era of the Waldorf-Astoria breakfast for Mrs. Woodrow Wilson, 1912.

By the 1920's slips and girdles were worn

Laguna Gloria hostess, 1932

Plate 9

(Courtesy, Sam Houston State University Library)

Soon after I paid the note on the headquarters building for the Texas Federation of Women's Clubs, Governor W. Lee O'Daniel proclaimed that Clara Driscoll Day be observed on October 4, 1939.

In 1929 Hal and I moved to Corpus Christi to manage the family ranch and other businesses. Some years later I deeded Laguna Gloria to the Texas Fine Arts Association for use as an art center and gallery. Half of my heart went out when I gave that home.

On a bluff overlooking Corpus Christi Bay I built a hotel and lived in its penthouse, visiting the ranch as often as my health allowed. How I loved the dogs and horses and cattle! I was always proud to call myself a cattlewoman.

Austin political meeting, 1928

Campaigning for John Nance Garner, 1940

Plate 10

I was interested in helping to shape a better state for Texans. For sixteen years I served as national Democratic Committeewoman from Texas. In 1933 President Roosevelt appointed Hal ambassador to Chile. In 1940 I supported John Nance Garner for President. When he did not gain the nomination, I backed President Roosevelt for a third term. In his 1941 inaugural parade I arranged for six pretty girls to ride white horses and for the Hardin-Simmons University Cowboy Band to march. Later in the week I gave a reception for the Texas delegation.

In April 1945 news came that President Roosevelt had died. Even though I did not agree with all of his policies, we were always political friends. At this time I was sixty-four years old. I thought not only of the late President but of how good life had been to me by offering opportunities to improve the lives of others.

Palo Alto "wagon wrench" cattle brand

Clara Driscoll died on July 17, 1945. Thousands of Texans came to pay their last respects to "the Savior of the Alamo" as her body lay in state in the beloved shrine she had rescued.

Spots, my faithful fox terrier

At Palo Alto Ranch

In her will Clara Driscoll provided for a children's hospital to be built in Corpus Christi. Medical care is available for all South Texas children.

Clara Driscoll did not write this story; however, the facts are taken from history.

To read more about her, the biography *Clara Driscoll: An American Tradition* by Martha Anne Turner is available at the Alamo Museum and in public libraries.

———

A royalty from sales of this book has been assigned to the Driscoll Children's Hospital, Corpus Christi, Texas.

The Robert Driscoll and Julia Driscoll and Robert Driscoll, Jr. Foundation graciously loaned all photographs reproduced, except those indicated.

CUTTING SUGGESTIONS:

1. Draw tabs on the shoulders, sides, and hats of the costumes.
2. Cut the blank face along the hairline down to the collar or necklace.
3. Leave some blank areas uncut for reinforcement.